MOST EMBARRASSING MOMENTS

The Worst Day Ever

by Joyce A. Barnes

illustrated by Matt Vincent

EMBARRASSED in Front of the World!

by Julia Campbell

GLOBE FEARON

Pearson Learning Group

CONTENTS

The Worst Day Ever

EMBARRASSED in Front of the World!

The Worst Day Ever

by Joyce A. Barnes
illustrated by Matt Vincent

CHAPTER 1 Off to a Great Start

An hour before my alarm was due to go off, I awoke with one thought in mind: *Today's my day! It's finally come!* I should have leaped out of bed, pumped up with energy, excited that my future was about to begin. Instead, I lay there, **absorbed** in feelings of doubt and watching the brightening sky for a sign.

My family's house that morning was eerily quiet, and I remembered that Mom and Dave, my stepfather, had already left to take my brother, Johnny, to basketball practice, while Grandma had gone to visit her sister. I was all alone with my thoughts, and my mood gradually shifted from doubt to fear. *What if you forget all your lines or can't do the dance? What if they cast someone else as the lead, and you end up in the chorus again?*

Two months ago, my high school drama teacher, Mr. Morgan, had surprised the class with an announcement. "Our new school play will be a musical, one all of you know and love—with some changes."

Mr. Morgan had paused for dramatic effect while we looked at him with anticipation. "Actually, we're going to write our own hip-hop musical. The story line will be an updated version of *Grease*, the story of how different groups of kids in a high school get together."

Various students chimed in with comments like "You've got to be joking!" and "A hip-hop musical?" Alice Johnson turned up her nose and said loudly, "It can't be done."

"It *can* be done, if we all work on this together. You're an **imaginative** group. I know we can write new, updated songs," Mr. Morgan continued, "and change the setting to a high school like ours. The story will include a TV dance contest, and we'll put a live emcee onstage."

"Can we hire a DJ?" asked Ricky Omari, who seemed to be caught up in Mr. Morgan's vision.

Mr. Morgan said confidently, "Why not?"

"We can dress in cool clothes, and I can work on costumes," Carmelita Perez enthusiastically suggested.

"Definitely," Mr. Morgan answered.

Everyone started talking at once. I just sat there, one thought on my mind: *I want to play the Sandy character.*

I've loved the musical *Grease* ever since I saw a local theater production in seventh grade, and I always imagined I could play Sandy well. Sandy gets to fall in love, she grows and changes and has the best solos, and she's the one the audience loves. I wanted to be that girl.

We decided to call the hip-hop musical *It's the Word*. I helped with the writing and **immersed** myself in everything about the Sandy character, whom we decided to call Shandi. I learned Shandi's lines and practiced her songs till the members of my family complained they could not get the words out of their heads.

My **persistence** paid off. Just yesterday, I learned I had made today's audition callbacks.

After today's callbacks, the major roles would be cast, so this was my last opportunity to win my dream role. *What if I don't get the part?* The troublesome question worried my mind **momentarily**, making it hard to climb out of bed. Yet when my clock radio clicked on at 6:15, I had to get up. Music always helps me get moving, so I turned up the volume and danced.

As far as dancing goes, all I can say is, I'm working on it. My friends had to teach me the audition moves, patiently and **persistently**, until I caught on. However, when I'm by myself, I dance like I'm in my own music video. When the song ended, I was revved up like an engine. I had **strengthened** my resolution to *really* make today my day.

Forty-five minutes later, I was frozen in a state of inaction, unable to decide what to wear to school. I had planned to dress in character as Shandi, to help me focus at the audition. However, I hadn't decided whether to dress like the Shandi in acts 1 and 2, the naïve goody-goody, or the Shandi at the end of the play, cool, bold, and ready for life.

I blinked at the clock; it was **crisis** time. The bus would arrive soon, and I had to get on it. If I missed the bus, I'd be late for school, and if I was late for school, I'd get detention. If I was in detention, I couldn't audition. So my future depended on making that bus!

I threw off my pajamas and pulled on my black jeans, a white T-shirt, and heels. With seconds to spare, a black leather-jacketed act 3 Shandi flew out the front door, complete with backpack. I spotted the idling school bus half a block away, so I made a mad dash for the stop.

Wearing my usual athletic shoes, I can run like a sprinter, but running in high heels is a dangerous feat. In the back window of the bus bobbed a row of faces, pointing and laughing as I plodded along. "Please tell him to wait," I yelled and waved, but the students in the back just laughed even harder. A puff of white smoke blew from the tailpipe as the bus started slowly pulling away.

I must have looked like a crazy earthbound bird, screaming and running and flailing my arms. I was gaining ground until one of my heels was caught in a crack in the pavement, and I stopped short and fell flat on the ground. Helpless, hurt, and out of breath, I watched the laughing kids recede into the distance. My chance to audition for Shandi, my big opportunity, was driving away.

As I lay on the ground, I thought, *If nothing is broken, I can still run all the way to school if I have to, if I just take off my shoes.* I warily stood, and after checking for pain (I was going to have some bruises, but nothing seemed to be broken), I started removing my heels. Suddenly, the bus jerked to a stop up ahead of me. For a moment, I couldn't believe my eyes. Then, I recognized some of my friends energetically waving from the back window. The bus was waiting for me, and my day was saved!

All I could manage was a brisk limp. As I got closer, I could hear laughter coming from inside the bus. I tried to ignore it, but as I stepped aboard, I heard the **supposedly** funny taunts being called down the aisle: "Hey, Kelly, did you think you could fly?" "If she were only a bird, instead of a Foxx!" My last name, Foxx, is often a punch line. Alice Johnson put in, "She may be a Foxx, but she's still a clown."

"Yuk, yuk, yuk," I responded, my face in a deep burn. The nickname Kelly the Clown gets on my nerves. I'd been trying to shake the clown label since I started high school, but some people who'd known me in middle school just couldn't give it up. Still, I couldn't blame them today because I probably did look funny running and falling and limping along.

Before I could thank the driver for waiting, he slammed the door shut behind me. "Be on time next time!" he growled and then sent the bus lurching forward so that I almost fell again.

Although my friends were beckoning from the back rows, I sank into a seat in an empty front row, unable to face the snickers behind me. All I wanted to do was to sit and be quiet. So I closed my eyes, took a deep breath, and tried to regain my Shandi-like cool.

Then, at the next stop, the seats next to me began to fill up with Tommy Sanders and his band of disorderly friends. Tommy is a year behind me in school, and I've known him all my life. Alone he is tolerable; with his friends, he's a **perpetual** teaser, and often, I'm the primary target. Was I **destined** to suffer more ridicule today, before I even made it to school?

"Hey, Kelly," he offered, sounding friendly enough. For Tommy, that was downright **subtle**. I answered him but held my breath. Tommy was like a firecracker: you never knew if he was going to pop off. Today, it seemed that he and his friends would leave me alone. Even the others had apparently moved on.

Closing my eyes once again, a thrilling vision entered my mind. I pictured myself on a graffiti-painted stage, dancing with a decked-out Jake Rocket, our name for the Danny Zuko character. In my version, however, there was no other girl character to sweep him away; instead, Jake and I won the break-dancing contest. I must admit, there's another reason why I wanted to get the part of Shandi. There was only one rapper in our entire school who could play the role of Jake Rocket and dance the moves and who rhymed the best, and that person was Oscar Clemente.

Oscar had moved to our city at the beginning of ninth grade. On his first day freshman year, he had stood out in the center of a rowdy crowd, already engaged in a contest with some other rappers. He was clearly the best, and after he won, he shook hands with his **rivals** and flashed his big million-dollar smile.

On this day that was so full of possibilities, I couldn't help wondering, *How strange would it be if Oscar played Jake and I was his girlfriend, Shandi, and life could imitate art for a change?*

Suddenly, I heard a low, hungry growl that seemed to have come from my stomach. At least I hoped it was low, but when I opened my eyes, I saw Tommy and his friends on the brink of hysteria. I'd left home with no time to eat, and now my stomach was complaining **noticeably**. "Grrrrrrr," it sounded again, this time very loudly.

Tommy pointed to me, wide-eyed with imaginary fear, calling to the driver, "Hey, stop the bus! There's a wild animal in here—I think it's a Foxx!" A fresh ripple of laughter broke out on the bus. *Kelly Foxx wows them again.* I joined in with the jokes, thinking, *If I keep them laughing, they will drown out the sound of my stomach!* My day just had to get better than this. How could it get any worse?

I hobbled into my first-period class, which was chemistry lab. Joey Iglesias, my lab partner, had already started setting up the assigned experiment. He had placed modeling clay on a metal tray and had stood a paper-clip hook upright in the middle of the clay. He was currently stapling together a tube made of cardboard and aluminum foil. When he looked up and saw me limping, his mouth and eyes formed big round O's. "What happened to you?" he asked.

"I did a dance with the pavement this morning," I said, trying to smile but grimacing instead. Incredibly, my clothes didn't have a smudge or a tear, and my wounded pride was somewhat healed. It was my ankle that was feeling the pain now. "It's a bruise or a sprain, that's all."

Joey got right to the relevant question and asked, "How will you dance at your audition if you can barely walk now?" He was one of the friends who had spent several weeks teaching me how to dance and choreographing my audition routine. Joey's expression **implied** that all his work had been in vain.

"My ankle will be fine if I just take it easy," I said.

"Would everyone please start your experiment," said Mrs. Kennedy, our chemistry teacher, giving us both an admonishing look.

"We'd better get started. You just sit and take notes. Read the instructions while I do the procedures. You can tell me what happened as we work," Joey advised. It seemed like a good plan. The assignment for the class sounded clear enough: to build a calorimeter and test the amount of energy in a marshmallow.

I had to resist the urge to eat the test subject, but I managed. The real problem was that we couldn't stop talking. We had become so **immersed** in our conversation that we lost track of what we were doing.

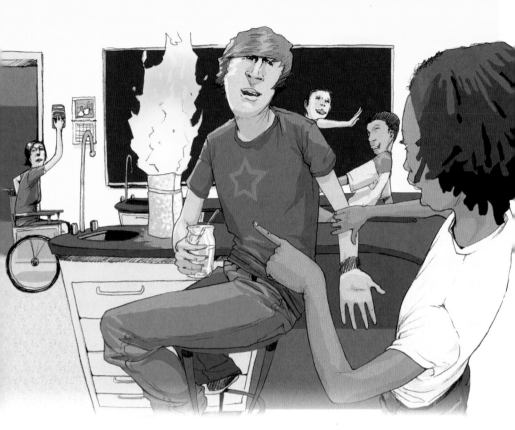

"Maybe the nurse can tape your ankle," Joey offered as he continued to follow the steps of the experiment, sticking a marshmallow on the paper-clip hook.

Pouring water into a beaker, I said, "My shoes are tight enough now."

Joey lit the marshmallow on three sides and then placed the cardboard-and-foil tube around the flame. He turned to face me and said, "Maybe she'll let you just sit in her office with an ice pack on your ankle."

I thought about that and then shook my head and said, "I don't think the sprain is that—baaad!"

I had noticed the smoke rising behind Joey seconds before a brilliant flame shot into the air. "Fire!" I yelled.

"Get out of the room, all of you," Mrs. Kennedy ordered as she pulled the alarm bell beside her desk and shooed us all out. She was the last to leave the room, wheeling herself out in her wheelchair and then closing the door behind her.

The hallway filled with bodies, moving excitedly toward the exits. "What happened?" someone shouted over the clanging. "Is there really a fire?" Joey and I kept quiet and moved away from the rest of the kids, too embarrassed to even speak to each other.

By the time the fire trucks arrived on the scene, the **crisis** was already over. The small flame had only burned **momentarily** and then had gone out.

We were lucky this time, but as added **insurance**, the firefighters checked the room to make sure no sparks had flown around to ignite another fire. This inspection took quite a while, so the whole school stood fidgeting outside for 20 minutes.

Joey and I had caused all this commotion. We kept our mouths shut, of course, but the story of who was responsible for the fire spread anyway. A group of kids discovered our hideout, and Joey and I glanced at each other and swallowed hard as the kids approached.

"Hey, Kelly, good job," one of them called out, **implying** that this had all been a big joke. "Thanks for the break, because we were taking a test."

"It was an accident," I answered.

"Oh, sure," another kid replied gleefully. "Kelly, you're such a clown."

"I wasn't clowning this time," I insisted, only it was no use. They slapped me on the back and walked away happy. Somehow, this made me even sadder. Was I **destined** to be a clown forever?

Back in class, Mrs. Kennedy was in no mood for laughing as she called Joey and me to the front of the room. I could only imagine what lay in store. Once again, I was facing detention. If Mrs. Kennedy thought we had been fooling around instead of doing our work, she might write us up for full suspension. What would my parents say? Here I was in so much trouble already on what was supposed to be my big day.

We told Mrs. Kennedy the truth about what we had done—or not done. "What should you have done with the beaker of water?" she shot at us.

"We should have placed it on top of the cylinder," I said.

"Why is that?" Mrs. Kennedy demanded.

"It would have starved the flame of oxygen."

"That's right—but instead, you two got distracted and nearly burned down the school. You could have caused terrible damage, not to mention harm to yourselves and others," Mrs. Kennedy angrily lectured us.

We had been tried and found guilty. I waited for our sentence with dread, kissing my precious audition goodbye. To our surprise, Mrs. Kennedy's anger diminished. "I know you both well," she stated sympathetically, "and this is not like you. I won't give you detention, but until I can trust you, you'll sit up front where I can keep watch. Do you understand?"

"Yes, ma'am, we do," we gratefully replied.

"You're just having a bad day," my friend Renée counseled me at lunch.

"What does that mean?" I asked. "That I'm doomed? Fine, I'll buy my **insurance** policy now."

Joey stopped by our table with a tray full of awful cafeteria food. "Don't listen to Renée," he told me. "You're having a bad *first half* of the day; that's all. Things will get better if you'll just be more careful."

"They have to get better," I said, planning to make sure that the rest of the day was trouble free—no more **crises**, falls, or fires. For lunch, I ate a neat, simple cheese sandwich and drank a small bottle of juice— nothing I might choke on. I tucked a napkin over my white T-shirt and put one across my lap for good measure.

"How is your ankle?" Renée asked.

"Actually, it doesn't hurt any more," I said. *Great*, I thought, *now I can stop worrying*. I needed to get back into character, to strut in as Shandi for the second audition and conquer my what-ifs once and for all. Having made it through lunch with no major mishaps, I now had to navigate my afternoon classes—math, English, and history. What harm could they do me?

Just then, Julie Stokes, my principal competition for the part of Shandi, walked into the cafeteria. I wondered if she was having a day anything like mine. **Momentarily**, I hoped that was true. Immediately, however, I **regretted** the thought. *Julie is nice*, I told myself. *She can't help that she's talented—and perfectly suited to play Shandi.*

"Hi, girls," she called in her Shandi-like way.

"Hi, Julie," we answered in unison.

"I'm so nervous about our audition today! How about you, Kelly?" she asked. She didn't look nervous at all.

"Oh, I'm doing great." Renée looked at me, but I shot her a frown and she understood.

"Well, good luck, then," Julie graciously offered, **perpetually** friendly.

Trying to mean it, I responded, "Same to you."

As soon as Julie was out of earshot, I burst out, "Oh, what was I thinking! They'll never cast me when Julie Stokes is Shandi all over. She's my biggest **rival**."

Renée tried to be supportive. "You've got a good chance—they liked your singing, and they called you back, so they know you can act. Just be extra careful."

I nodded and stood up to tiptoe to my next class. That's when I saw it, shiny and new, staring up at me from the linoleum floor: a penny for good luck, my **insurance** against any more problems! I couldn't resist. I bent down to get it and popped up in time to collide with a tray full of milk, chili, limp peas, and cherry pie.

"Look what you've done!" I bellowed at the boy carrying the tray, a freshman whose name I didn't know. I wanted to cry as I stood there dripping and hearing the meanest sound I could imagine—people laughing.

"I'm sorry!" the tray-carrying criminal stammered. "I didn't see you—oh, here, let me help you." He hastily grabbed up some napkins, but it was no use. Artistic splotches of brown and red now covered my T-shirt, and my black jeans were soaking wet.

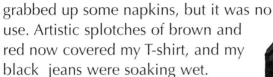

It wasn't the boy's fault, but I couldn't stop screaming. "I give up! It's impossible. I can't audition like this." I felt paralyzed by despair. By this time, no one was laughing at me, but I felt worse than I ever had in all my life. Renée took my arm and firmly led me out of the cafeteria.

"I'm really sorry," the boy called again. By now, I **regretted** yelling at him, but I was too filled with a crushing self-pity to apologize to him. Everything that I had wanted and worked for was doomed.

"It's hopeless," I moaned to Renée as she led me into the girls' locker room. "I can't leave school to go home and change, and then come back to audition. I don't have a way to get there and back. Last night, Mom and Dave both said how busy they were going to be today at work." My future looked unmistakably bleak.

"Go wash yourself off," Renée instructed me. "I have some exercise clothes in my locker that are sort of like regular clothes. We wear the same size, so you can put those on."

My hopes lifted. I definitely couldn't wear my own gym clothes, which consisted of a worn-out gray T-shirt and navy shorts that had seen better days, to the audition. I wondered what Renée's spare set of clothes looked like.

Renée returned bearing the clothes, and it was all I could do to not crumple right there. We wear the same size, yes, but I had never put on an outfit like this one—a pink, nubby sweat suit with lacy white trim. I stifled a hysterical laugh.

"No, no, no, I can't wear this for my audition," I blurted ungratefully.

"What choice do you have?" Renée asked, **noticeably** offended.

Staring helplessly at the unlikely costume, I wailed, "I'll look like a pink bunny hopping around."

Laughing, Renée said, "I'm sorry, Kelly, but you're so funny even in bad situations."

"I don't want to be funny! I'm tired of being everyone's joke. Kelly the Clown is all anyone knows," I said with a sigh.

I sank down on a bench. "How do you change your reputation, anyway? Renée, you know you get called the Brainiac sometimes; doesn't that bother you?"

"I know who I am—who cares what other people say?" Renée answered calmly. "I *am* smart, and being called the Brainiac doesn't hurt me. It just makes other people look dumb because it shows that they only see one thing about me."

I'd hoped to get sympathy from Renée, but I wasn't going to get it.

"You should have the same attitude," she continued. "You're not *just* a clown. Maybe you were that way in middle school, but you're different now. You're into acting, and you study hard. You're still funny, though, and maybe you should appreciate that about yourself instead of trying to fight it."

I blinked, trying to take in her words.

"Now, please try on this sweat suit," Renée urged. "What you're wearing is not as important as what you do when you get on that stage. Mr. Morgan will still see what a good performer you are."

I looked at Renée gratefully. Some people might call her the Brainiac, but I called her my friend.

As I cleaned up, I had time to consider all that had happened so far. I'd fallen in front of a whole busload of people, but nothing was broken. Some students thought I was playing a joke when I almost set the school on fire. Yet Mrs. Kennedy had understood and had given me a break, and I knew I'd never be so foolishly careless again. I had made a great fuss in the cafeteria. Of all my embarrassing moments today, I remembered that one with the most **regret**. I needed to find the boy who had held the tray and apologize for yelling at him.

Despite everything, I could still hope that things would work out right. What might seem on the surface as **perpetual** bad luck could also be seen in a positive light.

I put on the bunny suit and returned for inspection. This time, Renée laughed heartily. "I'm glad you find me so hilarious," I said. "Instead of auditioning for a hip-hop *Grease*, maybe I should go for the *pink* rock version."

Renée fell on the floor. Laughter's contagious, and soon both of us were holding our stomachs. When we recovered, Renée decided that if I was going to wear pink, I should still wear my black jacket. "You'll look like both sides of the Shandi character—innocent and ready to rumble."

"I'll look like a clown," I complained.

Renée is **persistent** when she wants to be. "You know, I have sneakers that will look better with that sweat suit than your heels."

Renée's black sneakers turned out to have polka-dot laces, and they were an inch too big for me, so I walked with a flop. "If I can go out there in this bunny suit, I can do anything," I declared.

"That's right," Renée cheered.

"Julie Stokes or no Julie Stokes, I can play Shandi!"

"You said it!" she yelled back.

With a friend like that, I couldn't give up. "Here I come, audition—bring it on!"

CHAPTER 6

Kelly's Got Skills

I made it through my afternoon classes with no further mishaps. My success **strengthened** my resolve. Feeling more confident than I had felt all day, I walked into the small auditorium where the auditions would be held. In the darkened room, some students sat speaking together in low voices, whereas others meditated alone. I guessed they were trying to "get into character," to think and feel like the characters they were auditioning for.

Mr. Morgan and Mrs. Oliver, our music teacher, sat at a table in front. I signed in and took a seat near them, pulling off the leather jacket.

A noisy group entered with Julie and Oscar. The group sat in a clump near the back, where someone began making beat-boxing sounds.

This kid was good—the beats and rhythms coming out of his mouth made me want to get up and dance. Soon enough, Oscar and other auditioning students started trading rhymes back and forth; some lines were from the play, others were freestyle. These students were warming up, which is what I should have been doing as well. Instead, I tried to remain unnoticed.

Renée popped in at the back door. "Psssst, Kelly," she hissed, motioning me to follow her. I glanced at the Oscar crowd as if I were checking the street before crossing. With the **subtlety** of a stampede across the plains, I flopped in my big white shoes toward the exit.

"Hey, Kelly!" Oscar called out. I looked up, alarmed, and then stopped in my tracks when he flashed his million-dollar smile—a costly mistake.

"Kelly's got it all mixed up," Oscar said to the beat, "and she looks kinda funny. She heard this was a hip-hop play and came dressed like a bunny."

A wave of approval for Oscar's rhyme swept through the crowd. I wanted to run out of there, go home, forget about Shandi and Jake Rocket, forget about the show, forget about wanting to act at all. I longed to disappear in a puff of pink bunny smoke. Surprisingly, however, I wheeled around to face him.

"A bunny is quick, a bunny is smart," I said back to him, "and don't forget, I'm also a Foxx. I'm sly and I'm slick and can pick you apart, from your precious teeth right down to your socks."

This time, the students cheered for me. "Kelly's got skills," someone called, and Oscar laughed, too. "You got me that time," he acknowledged, yet that didn't keep him from making up more rhymes at my expense. It was all in fun, no harm intended, but every new line was a stab to my heart. My vision blurred, and each laughing face seemed to become a bouncing balloon. The shouts and laughs echoed through my bones.

I could not let them see how much I hurt, so I stood there joking along with the others. All they saw was Kelly the Clown. What do you do with a clown? You laugh. How could I show them, or Mr. Morgan and Mrs. Oliver, my serious side, that I could play a dramatic lead, if a clown was all they could see?

Once again, Renée came to my rescue, calling and waving from the auditorium door. "Kelly, come on."

Turning toward Mr. Morgan, I said, "Is it okay if I leave for a few minutes?"

"Sure, " he said, "but don't take too long. You've signed up to sing the role of Shandi, and you're third on the list."

"Yes, sir," I managed to say and crept out of the room on unsteady feet. My plan was to escape under the pretense of going with Renée. Once out of her sight, I would run out of the school and all the way home.

"Never mind those kids," Renée said once we were in the hallway. "Remember what I told you before: all that counts is what you do when you get on that stage." Her words made so much sense that I wanted to believe them, even though the idea of standing in front of that crowd and singing or dancing seemed impossible now.

"You've got to be joking—I can't go back in there," I mumbled.

"Come on, Kelly—don't give up yet. I'm counting on you to show everyone what a star you are."

A lump formed in my throat as I listened to my one-member fan club. With a friend like that, I wanted to believe I still had a chance. Once more, I rallied to restore my hope.

"Now, let's see," Renée said, consulting her watch, "Joey should be here any second."

"Why?" I asked.

"We're going to rehearse your dance moves."

"Fine," I said, sighing, "it can't hurt."

Joey seemed to be running late, so Renée spent the time arranging my hair, gathering it all in one giant ponytail on top of my head. Then, she let the strands fall in every direction. The hairstyle looked good, but if I turned the wrong way, hair fell in my eyes.

"I didn't think of that," Renée admitted. "Just try not to move the wrong way; there isn't time to do it over."

Joey ran up to us, out of breath. "Sorry. I had to see a teacher about making up a test I missed when I was sick last week." He did a double take when he saw my outfit. "Kelly, what are you wearing?"

"A pink bunny suit," I answered him. "It's Renée's."

"Okay." Joey took a deep breath. "Come on, let's see your dance."

"Just like that, I'm supposed to dance?" I complained. "Without any music?"

"We'll sing." Joey started humming the tune of my song. I guess he couldn't tell how off-key he was, but Renée and I started to laugh.

Folding his arms, Joey complained, "What are you laughing about? Are you **implying** that I can't sing?"

"Sorry," Renée apologized. "It's just that Kelly was having a **crisis**, and I don't think we're helping her much."

"I'll tell you what a **crisis** is," I informed them. "It will be when I miss my scheduled audition time because my **supposedly** helpful friends are making me late. Okay, I'd better get back in the auditorium—thanks for cheering me up."

"Wait a second!" Renée ordered. She tried tying the polka-dot laces to make the shoes fit more snugly. "Oh, no, this one just broke!"

"Great. Now my sneaker will fly off while I'm dancing and knock someone right in the head!" I flopped into the auditorium just in time to grab my black jacket.

Mr. Morgan looked up as I entered the room. "There you are, Kelly. I was just about to call your name. You're on next."

I scrambled onto the stage and took my place. The music began, and I started to sing the words to my song: "How can you tell when your future begins? Who's there to tell you, 'Today is the day?'" My voice sounded raspy and cracked on the high notes. My throat felt raw. Screaming to catch the bus in the morning and yelling during my lunchtime meltdown had strained my vocal cords. I had to drop down an octave to sing the song.

As I danced, I turned my head so my hair wouldn't fall in my face and kept the shoe with the broken lace glued to the floor so it wouldn't fall off. I knew I must have looked strange, but I kept moving.

Subtle sounds of laughter floated up from the rows of seats, making me more nervous. I could feel my movements becoming even more jerky. Somehow, I made it to the end of the song with both shoes still on.

"That was fine," Mr. Morgan said, smiling. He consulted with Mrs. Oliver for a moment and then announced, "We'd like you to sing one other song: Roz's big number."

I'm sure my shock was **noticeable**. Roz's song—why that one? Roz was what we'd called the Rizzo character in our musical—the girl who made everyone laugh. In the story, she was the total opposite of Shandi.

I finally spoke. "I'm a little hoarse today. I can usually sing Shandi's solos just fine."

Mr. Morgan said, "That's okay, Kelly. We like how you sound. We just want to hear you sing this song. Do you know the words?"

"Um—" I stammered. I'd certainly heard the song several times, but I'd been so **immersed** in learning Shandi's solos that I'd paid little attention to Roz's. "Sure, I can sing that," I finally told them. What else could I do but give it a try?

Sure enough, in some places I forgot the words, so I started to freestyle over the beats. I'd fill in with rhymes I made up on the spot, making them as **imaginative** as I could. Now and then, I'd go back to the lyrics as written. After I had finished singing the song, the two teachers clapped. "Kelly, you're a natural," Mrs. Oliver said, beaming.

I wondered what that remark meant as I walked off the stage. Joey and Renée were waiting outside the auditorium. "How'd you do?" they asked.

"**Supposedly**, I'm a natural," I said.

"A natural what?" Joey wanted to know.

A natural loser was what I was thinking. All that was left was to go home and live the whole day over, for surely, the first words from my family would be, "How did it go, Kelly?"

"This was the most embarrassing day I've ever had," I told my family as we got ready for dinner. "I wish I could just start over, that this day had never happened."

Dave popped his head into the room. "Kelly, it couldn't have been *that* bad," he said, **implying** that I was exaggerating, as I've been known to do.

"You want to bet?" I retorted. "Tell me if you've ever had a day like this." I started at the beginning and told them how I'd woken up early and then almost missed the bus. I acted out the scenes from the day, including the dangerous chemistry incident, determined to tell them every horrifying detail.

Grandma sat at the dining room table, listening to my tragic tale, while Mom and Dave cooked dinner and made sympathetic noises. Johnny helped me set the table, even though it wasn't his turn. Who better to complain to than those who love you no matter what?

Finally, I got to the audition disaster. "You should have seen me up on that stage, trying to keep my hair out of my face and my right shoe from flying away." I showed them some moves from my modified routine and wasn't surprised when they all started laughing.

"Renée and Joey were no help," I announced. I imitated Joey's singing my song and Renée's breaking my shoelace. Soon, I had my family falling apart.

"Kelly," Mom giggled, "you're such a good mimic, so **imaginative**, that I can picture it all just as you tell it."

"She's a good actress, too," Dave put in. "I still say your day turned out well. You **persisted** through all of those problems, and I'm proud of you, Kel."

Grandma nodded her head. "Tell me more about the musical *Spread the Word*."

"We're calling the show *It's the Word*," I answered, laughing. I explained how we wrote new songs for the show and how much I wanted to be cast as Shandi. "Mr. Morgan and Mrs. Oliver clapped after I sang, but for the wrong song. What does that mean? Do you think I have a shot at getting the role I really want?"

Nobody answered at first. I looked at them, hoping they would make me feel better, as if their words could be **insurance** against my botched audition.

Mom, who had been standing in the doorway of the dining room, came and stood beside me. "Kelly," she said, "you did your best even with all the problems you had. Now, the producers will make their decision. You'll just have to wait and see what they say—that's the actor's life."

Grandma added, "Your mother is right. Today, you showed whether you can handle being an actor: the wanting, the waiting, the chance you will get the part you think you're **destined** to have—and the chance you won't."

I sat at the table, **absorbing** all my family had said. *What if* crept back into my mind, and I wondered what kind of actor I'd be if I couldn't handle this part of the deal.

Perhaps this day had been a test, a way to **strengthen** my endurance for what was to come. Maybe this day had been meant to convince me that I don't have what it takes to pursue an actor's life—the life I'd dreamed of since middle school. For the first time, I started to realize that there is more to that life than what happens onstage.

Hugging me, Mom said, "We're pulling for you no matter what." Everyone agreed, including Johnny.

"What does it matter which part you get?" he said. "You'll end up stealing the show anyway."

I got up to hug him. During the meal, as talk swirled around me, I thought about how much my family's steady reassurance **strengthened** me. Once I'd had a minor role in a show called *Brigadoon*. I was the first one onstage, welcoming everyone to the fair and then retreating into the crowd of townspeople onstage. Yet Dave had stood with his camera looking as proud as any parent could be, and Mom had bragged to all the relatives about my wonderful performance. Afterward, they'd given me a dozen red roses as if I were some Broadway star.

I pictured them sitting in the audience for *It's the Word*, rooting for me even if, again, I was part of the chorus. That picture made the idea that I might not get a lead role bearable.

That night, however, as I lay in bed, I envisioned myself singing Shandi's songs the way I had rehearsed them, not the way I had performed in my audition. Despite all the good advice from my family and friends, I realized, I still wanted to be Shandi.

The alarm woke me up at 6:15. With no hesitation, I hopped out of bed as the familiar sounds of my family's morning routine filtered into my room. "Johnny, if you don't hurry up, you'll be late" was followed by the grumbled reply, "I'm coming already!" and "Where are my keys? Can you help me find my keys?" After a hearty breakfast, I walked to the bus stop. The driver smiled when I got on, and I smiled back. All was forgiven. So far, I hadn't said one thing to anyone about *It's the Word*. I talked with my friends about ordinary topics, pretending that this was just another day. Yet the whole time, my stomach quivered like a leaf in a thunderstorm, and my feet kicked the floor of the bus, trying to make it go faster.

When I finally arrived at school, I found Joey and Renée waiting for me at the main entrance. I was grateful to see them, but by then, I could hardly utter a proper "hello." Together, we walked toward Mr. Morgan's office, where we knew the cast list would be posted on the door. We saw other students already gathered around the list.

I took some deep breaths, and Renée gave me a wink of assurance. As we drew closer, I saw Julie Stokes, who looked at me and then broke into a smile. *What is she trying to tell me?* I wondered. *We can't both have gotten the part.* When Julie waved eagerly, I suddenly felt faint.

A few steps more would put me in front of the cast list. In the meantime, I had to keep walking along a corridor of students who all seemed to be staring at me, no doubt waiting to break into laughter when they saw me react to the list.

Finally, I was close enough to read the paper on the door.

"Jake Rocket—Oscar Clemente." No surprise there. "Shandi—Julie Stokes."

My heart stopped pumping and turned to stone. Was I moaning out loud?

Julie shook my limp, numb hand. "Congratulations!" she chirped. "We're in this play together: me as Shandi and you as Roz!"

I couldn't conceal my shock. Julie didn't seem to notice my reaction, but my friends watched me closely. "Roz is my favorite character," Renée gently commented. I shook my head, feeling so disappointed that I couldn't speak.

Just then, Mr. Morgan opened his door. "Congratulations," he said to Julie and me. "We have a wonderful cast. Kelly, this is your first lead role. You certainly showed all of us how—"

Don't say the word! I screamed inside, squeezing my eyes shut. *I can't bear to hear it, not today, not now. Please don't tell me I'm a clown.*

"You showed us just how talented you are," Mr. Morgan said.

My eyes flew open. *Talented? Me?*

I managed to reply, "Thanks, Mr. Morgan."

"We'll see you both at rehearsal tomorrow," he said before ducking back into his office.

Julie said, "I'm glad I'll be working with you, Kelly."

"Thanks, Julie. Oh, and congratulations—you'll make a great Shandi." Julie's good wishes were so sincere that somehow, my feelings of **rivalry** with her had vanished.

Just then, Oscar and some other students joined us. They read the whole list before Oscar shouted, "All right!" and slapped five with a boy I'd never noticed before.

"Good job, Julie. Kelly, I knew you'd get a good role," Oscar said. "Hey, have you met Shawn?" He introduced the boy I didn't know. "He's playing Chaz, the Kenickie character. You'll have a lot of scenes with him."

Shawn and I smiled at each other. *Where has he been hiding?* I wondered.

Julie suggested, "Let's meet at my house after school. We can try out some of our scenes, just for fun."

"Sounds good to me," Oscar replied.

"I'm in," Shawn agreed.

Julie looked at me expectantly. *Me*—spending the afternoon getting to know my cute, new onstage boyfriend? "Sure, count me in," I said casually.

Later, in study hall, I reread our script, concentrating on Roz's part. I was **absorbed** by her character. When I had finished, I felt sure I could play her role well—and love it. Like Shandi, Roz falls in love, grows, and changes.

Of course, I thought, *how much a character develops in the course of a drama isn't the only thing that makes a good role. So much depends on the actor who plays the character.* I'd grown, too, in just one day, as embarrassing as the day had seemed at the time.

The words to Shandi's song came back to me: *How can you tell when your future begins?* I suppose any day you learn something new about yourself is a day when your future begins. Mine had begun.

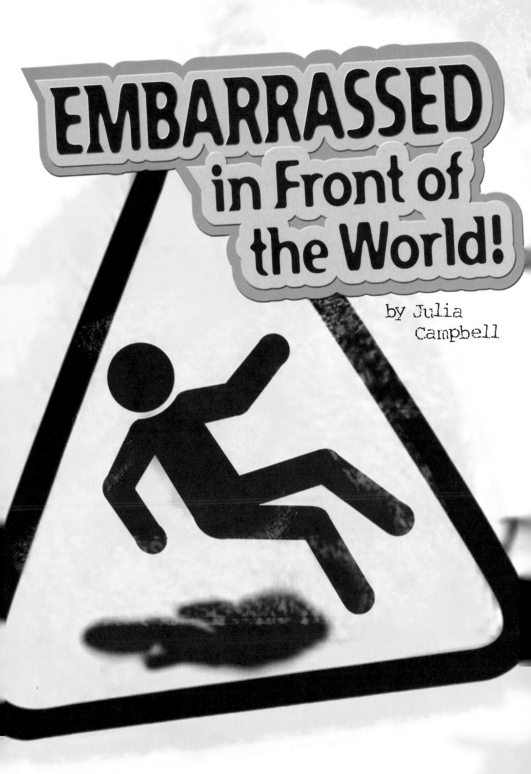

EMBARRASSED
in Front of
the World!

by Julia Campbell

Chapter 1
How Embarrassing!

Life can be so embarrassing sometimes. Everything can be going smoothly, and then, BAM! You forget the words you were going to say. You trip and fall in front of a room full of people. You say or do something really stupid when you're trying to impress someone. You drop the ball on a really big play. Embarrassing situations can **arise** from out of nowhere.

Do you remember the last time you did something really embarrassing? Did it just make you want to crawl under your bed and stay there? Now imagine your **anguish** if you did it while the whole world was watching. What if your embarrassing moment was caught on camera and forever recorded so people could watch you do that same thing over and over again? As you are about to find out, you wouldn't be the first person to whom this has happened. All of the people you're going to read about have firsthand knowledge of how embarrassing life can sometimes be.

The embarrassing moments in this selection have been divided into five categories: messing up words, public accidents, microphone follies, caught on camera, and sports bloopers. All of the people you'll read about were famous before their embarrassing moment. **Unfortunately** for them, the whole world was able to see their embarrassment.

You will read about political figures, famous singers, a news anchor, and sports stars. What binds these people together? Each of them was caught in an embarrassing moment. So the next time you do something embarrassing, remember that things could be worse. The whole world could be watching!

Chapter 2
That's Not What I Meant to Say

Does speaking in front of people **petrify** you? It can be very scary knowing that everyone is looking right at you! When you're in the spotlight, you may get nervous and stumble over even the easy words. Your mind could just go blank, and you could forget what you wanted to say.

As with most people, you'll probably have to speak in front of a group at some point in your life. You might have to give a book report or a speech at school. You might run for class president and have to speak in front of your entire class. You might have to give a toast at a wedding. It's okay if just thinking about speaking in front of people makes you nervous. As a matter of fact, speaking before an audience makes most people a little nervous. Some people even find public speaking **petrifying.**

Usually, everything turns out fine, though. As long as you prepare yourself beforehand, you'll probably be pleasantly surprised at how good you are at speaking in front of people. It's like most things in life: Practice makes perfect. You can practice in front of a mirror. You can practice in front of your family and friends. Practice will help you overcome your nervousness.

Sometimes no matter how much preparation and practice people do before speaking in public, embarrassing moments happen. People may misuse or mispronounce words or say something that simply doesn't make sense. In this chapter, you will read how a sports figure, a political figure, and a pop star messed up words when speaking in public.

A Special Way With Words

Have you ever heard of Yogi Berra? Yogi (Lawrence Peter) Berra played professional baseball for 19 seasons. He played as a catcher for the New York Yankees from 1946 to 1963 and for the New York Mets in 1965. As a Yankee, Yogi played on the winning team in 10 World Series. That is just one of the many amazing records he holds as a ballplayer, yet Yogi is almost as famous for what he has said off the field as for what he has done on it.

Yogi has a special and funny way with words. Many of his sayings sound pretty mixed up when you first hear them. Sometimes his grammar is a little mixed up, too. If you think about Yogi's sayings for a little while, however, you realize that he is expressing something valuable and wise. Here are some examples of Yogi's mixed-up sayings:

◇ *Nobody goes there anymore. It's too crowded.*

◇ *A nickel ain't worth a dime anymore.*

◇ *It gets late early out here.*

◇ *It ain't over 'til it's over.*

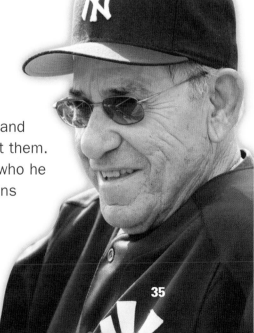

Some people would be very embarrassed if they uttered mixed-up sentences like these, but not Yogi! He has a sense of humor about his verbal "errors" and doesn't mind being teased about them. Yogi's sayings are just a part of who he is, and his family, friends, and fans love him for them!

Yogi Berra was both a player and ➡ manager for the New York Yankees.

Did He Just Say What I Think He Said?

John Fitzgerald Kennedy was the thirty-fifth president of the United States. Kennedy was president from 1961 until 1963, when he was assassinated. In June 1963, President Kennedy had to give an important speech in West Berlin, West Germany. At the time, Berlin was a divided city. West Berlin was democratic, whereas East Berlin was Communist. In 1961, the East German government, supported by the government of the Soviet Union (now called Russia), built an **ominous** wall that divided the city in half.

The East German government built the Berlin Wall to stop people from their side, East Berlin, fleeing to West Berlin. The Berlin Wall was a **dismal** reminder of the cold war. The cold war was a **treacherous** rivalry between the United States and the Soviet Union and its allies.

So it was a **dramatic** moment for President Kennedy on June 26, 1963, when he stood before 120,000 Germans in West Berlin to tell them that the United States government supported the West German government. President Kennedy was young, charming, and popular. The audience adored him and cheered wildly when he stepped onstage to speak.

President Kennedy spoke mostly in English until his last words. "Ich bin ein Berliner," he told the crowd. What he should have said was "Ich bin Berliner." "Ich bin Berliner" means "I am a Berliner." "Ich bin ein Berliner" can mean "I am a jelly doughnut"! Still, West Berliners knew what Kennedy meant to say and cheered him anyway. They understood that President Kennedy was declaring that the United States stood with West Berlin in its fight against the East German government.

Yum!

The Pop Star and Her Tuna Fish

Political figures are not the only ones who mess up words. Pop stars, whose lives are as public as those of political figures, put their foot in their mouth from time to time. Take pop star Jessica Simpson, for instance. Her CDs have sold millions of copies worldwide. In 2003, she starred in a show on MTV called *Newlyweds*.

Simpson has been called sweet and down-to-earth. In fact, Simpson said the reason her fans love her is that she's a pretty normal girl. "I'm just comfortable in my own skin, working the crowd and making jokes and just being silly—being who I am." The **consequences** of Simpson's silliness, however, are that she has frequent embarrassing moments and seems a bit mixed-up at times.

The television show *Newlyweds* was about what it's like to be young and married. The cameras recorded Simpson as she and her husband went about their everyday lives. Sometimes things got a little **absurd**. Simpson is shown mispronouncing French words and stumbling over English words like *dissemination* and *subsequent*.

In one episode, Simpson was offered Buffalo wings (spicy chicken wings named after the city of Buffalo, New York), and she replied, "I don't eat buffalo!"

Her most famous speaking goof had to do with a can of tuna. One night as Simpson sat and picked at her meal, she wondered aloud what "chicken of the sea" really was. "Is this chicken what I have, or is it fish?" she asked her husband, whose attention was focused on a sports show on television. The can was labeled Chicken of the Sea®.

Simpson said later she just got mixed up. "I knew it was tuna fish," she explained. "I was just really confused because I liked it, and I hate fish, and I thought for a split second there, it might be chicken."

Simpson admits she is "definitely ditzy." "I am the one who went and sang at the White House in front of President George W. Bush and messed the words up to 'God Bless America,'" Simpson says. "But I'm the kind of person that will like fall down a whole flight of stairs and get up and just say, 'I'm a dork.' If you call that kind of personality a ditz, then I guess I kind of take that as a compliment because it means I'm free-spirited."

"Everyone has their moments when they stick their foot in their mouth," Simpson says. At least Simpson has a good sense of humor about messing up words every now and then.

All of the **ordeals** you just read about are proof that even famous people make verbal errors at times. No matter how **absurd** the situation is, it's not the end of the world. Everyone gets embarrassed sometimes.

Jessica Simpson onstage

Chapter 3
Accidents Happen

You're rushing to get to class on time, and then, WHAM! You trip on the stairs and fall headfirst. On another occasion, it's snowing and you're late for the school bus. You have the **misfortune** of slipping on a patch of ice. You fall on the sidewalk, sending the contents of your backpack flying all over the place. Worse yet, it happens right in front of school with all your classmates watching. On another occasion, you're having lunch in the school cafeteria when suddenly you feel very sick and throw up! As luck would have it, the person you have a crush on is there to witness the event. It's bad enough to feel so ill, but embarrassment is an even bigger part of your misery.

All these situations are embarrassing, right? If something like this happens to you, how does it make you feel? At first, you may feel humiliated and miserable. You probably think you could die from embarrassment, but you live to laugh about it later.

Well now, think how much worse it would be if you were someone who is in the public eye. Every step—or misstep—famous people take is seen by thousands of people. In this chapter, you will read about a famous singer and two political figures whose embarrassing missteps were caught on camera. These well-known people have the **misfortune** of having to relive their embarrassing moments because they are seen again and again in newspapers and magazines and on television.

40

Watch Your Step, Miss Ross!

Diana Ross is a famous singer who was part of the 1960s musical group the Supremes. The group sold millions of albums. The Supremes had 12 number-one hit songs and sometimes competed for spots on the Billboard music charts with another really famous group of the 1960s, the Beatles.

Diana Ross was the lead singer for the Supremes. In 1970, she decided to launch a solo career. As a solo artist, Ross continued to produce hit song after hit song. During her career, she has been nominated for 12 Grammy Awards.

Because Ross has been a superstar for more than 40 years, she has become used to being the center of attention. At times, the attention has revolved around a new hit song she has just released. At other times, the attention has revolved around her latest world tour. With all of this attention, it's only natural that if something embarrassing happens to Ross, someone will probably be there to see and record it.

Diana Ross has enjoyed a long ⇥ and very successful career.

Ross is a big star with a special voice, but when it comes to standing on her own two feet, the superstar has faced a few challenges. Back in 1994, Ross was all set to sing at the World Cup (a big soccer tournament) in London, England. Just as she was headed onstage, Ross caught her heel on the hem of her gown and tripped, falling down. The audience gasped. Ross was **escorted** offstage and returned minutes later wearing a pantsuit. The show must go on, and fortunately the star suffered only a few bruises. Ross at least had a sense of humor about her mishap. She told her fans, "I'm falling for you."

Then in 2001, Ross was out with her children when a celebrity photographer began taking pictures of her. Ross wasn't happy about it. She took off one shoe and began chasing the photographer down the street. **Unfortunately**, the star tripped with her shoe still in her hand. The photographer was determined to get his picture and started snapping away while Ross was sprawled on the ground. The pictures later ran in a tabloid newspaper.

In 2002, Ross tripped again at an event at the National Tennis Centre in Melbourne, Australia. She tore her dress as she was **escorted** to the stage. Still, she was able to perform.

In March 2004, Ross took another tumble. As she was getting out of her limousine and preparing to make a **dramatic** entrance to a London awards show, Ross lost her balance. Fortunately, a bodyguard caught Ross midfall and she wasn't hurt. Through the years, Ross has certainly had one **ordeal** after another. Some of these situations were probably embarrassing for Ross, but she didn't let them stop the show from going on.

Presidential Candidate Flips for Votes

While on campaign, politicians sometimes do **absurd** things for publicity. If an opportunity **arises** that can help a candidate win a few votes, why not take it? So it was not unusual for Gary Bauer, a candidate in the 2000 presidential race, to enter a pancake-flipping contest.

Bauer, a Republican, was going up against better-known candidates such as George W. Bush, who was the governor of Texas at the time. Bauer needed a strong showing in the New Hampshire primary in order to have a chance to run for the presidency. The New Hampshire primary usually is a strong indicator of who will be the Republican and Democratic candidates for the national election. According to polls of voters, Bauer was in last place among the five people trying to be the Republican candidate for president.

On the day before the big primary vote, Bauer went to a campaign event in Manchester, New Hampshire. He joined a contest to see who could flip a pancake the highest using only a frying pan. Bush had joined the contest, too. Bauer tossed a pancake high into the air. **Unfortunately**, he miscalculated where it would land.

As the pancake started to fall, Bauer stepped back to try to catch it in his frying pan and tumbled off the 4-foot stage. Believe it or not, he managed to hop to his feet as the pancake landed back in his pan. Bauer later explained that since Bush had already caught his pancake, he wasn't going to be beaten and miss his big catch. However, catching the pancake didn't save Bauer from a **dismal** last place in the New Hampshire primary, whereas George W. Bush wound up winning the 2000 presidential election.

43

Presidential Mishap

Have you ever gotten sick to your stomach and thrown up in school or another public place? Throwing up is never pleasant, but when it happens in public, you can suffer from embarrassment, too. **Unfortunately**, throwing up often takes us by surprise. We can't always plan ahead so that we are in a private place when this kind of situation **arises**.

Of course, this kind of unpleasant surprise can happen to anyone. Consider, though, how much more embarrassing it would be to throw up in public if you were a guest at a formal dinner and the eyes of the world were on you. That's exactly the situation that former president George H. W. Bush found himself in.

President Bush visited Japan in January 1992 to discuss trade with Japanese prime minister Kiichi Miyazawa. During a formal state dinner, the president suddenly became ill. He threw up on the prime minister and then fainted. Videotaped pictures of the event were seen all over the world.

When a president of the United States becomes ill, it is news throughout the world. Interest in a U.S. president's health is **considerably** high not just in the United States but also in many other countries. People wanted to know if the president was seriously ill or just struck by an unpleasant but minor illness.

Fortunately, President Bush's problem was nothing more than a 24-hour flu. He made a speedy recovery and was able to talk to reporters about the episode the next day. President Bush answered the reporters' questions about his illness and explained that doctors had conducted tests and found nothing wrong with him.

How did President Bush handle this embarrassing situation? He discussed it openly and with a sense of humor. He reminded reporters that a **considerable** number of people in the United States had had the same 24-hour flu and jokingly asked, "So why isn't the president entitled to 24 hours?"

President Bush is a Republican. In 1992, he was facing reelection. So a reporter asked the president if he thought Democrats might suggest that his illness was a sign that he was not in good physical shape. His good-humored reply was that even Democrats get the flu from time to time.

President Bush may have thought that the best way to reassure people was to speak openly about getting sick. He probably also thought that laughing about an embarrassing situation is a good way to handle it. So if you should ever get sick to your stomach in a public place, here's a suggestion. Remind yourself that honesty and good humor helped the president of the United States handle the same embarrassing situation. They will probably work for you, too!

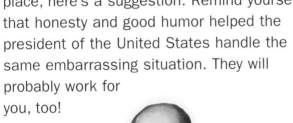

Prime Minister
Miyazawa
and President
George H. W. Bush
➡

Student "Picks" for Most Embarrassing Moment

◇ Giving the wrong answer to a teacher's question

◇ Having your "crush" overhear you talking about him or her

◇ Throwing up in front of everyone

◇ Tripping and falling down in front of the whole class

◇ Being overheard by someone you are complaining about

◇ Being scolded by a teacher in front of your classmates

◇ Having your pants fall down

◇ Calling the teacher "Mom"

◇ Spilling food all over yourself

Yikes!
I hate when →
that happens!

Chapter 4
Is This Microphone On?

Testing. One. Two. Three. Testing. You're getting ready to make a big speech. You have to use a microphone so everyone can hear you. There's a little button on the side that turns the microphone off and on. Most speakers do a sound check just to make sure it's working properly.

What if the microphone works when you don't want it to? What if the microphone is actually on when you think it is off? What if you're playing around and you say something that's not so nice? What if you reveal something you don't want anyone else to hear? People can sometimes say improper things when they don't think anybody is listening in.

Television news anchors and politicians speak into microphones all the time so people can hear what they're saying. They know it's important to be ready for their big moment. They know everyone will be listening to what they have to say. They know their words will be broadcast on the radio or on television or through speakers at a live event.

Did you ever wonder what those people say once the microphone is off? Well, sometimes the microphone is on when they think it's off. Oops. Famous people have told jokes and criticized other people while the world was listening in! In one case you'll read about, the joke could have had serious **consequences.** All of the people described in this chapter learned the hard way that checking the microphone before speaking can prevent stumbling into a very embarrassing situation.

News Anchor Calls the President a "Bore"

ABC news anchor David Brinkley was on television for many years. He started in Washington, D.C., the nation's capital, at the age of 23 and covered press conferences in the office of President Franklin Delano Roosevelt, who was president during World War II.

In 1956, Brinkley and his partner Chet Huntley became the country's first television evening news team. They called their show on NBC *The Huntley-Brinkley Report*. It was on the air for 14 years. In 1980, Brinkley left NBC to go to a competing network, ABC. He had his own show called *This Week With David Brinkley*. He interviewed lots of powerful people, including several presidents. He won ten Emmy Awards for his journalism. He was also awarded the Presidential Medal of Freedom in 1992.

David Brinkley was on television every night reporting the news. On the evening of the 1996 presidential election, he made a big mistake on the air, perhaps because he was very tired and **frustrated** as a result of working many long hours. News anchors work unusually long hours on Election Day. Brinkley had been on the air for about 8 hours by the time he was ready to stop reporting on election night in November 1996.

It was 1:30 in the morning. President Bill Clinton had just been reelected by the citizens of the United States. Brinkley was waiting for the cameras to start rolling. He didn't realize his microphone was still on and he was on live television! ABC news anchor Peter Jennings and other ABC correspondents were summing up the day's events. Brinkley thought the network had taken a commercial break.

Peter Jennings and David Brinkley
reporting on the 1996 election results

"We all look forward with great pleasure to four years of wonderful, inspiring speeches, full of wit, poetry, music, love, and affection, plus more nonsense," Brinkley said on camera. Jennings told him, "You can't say that on the air, Mr. Brinkley." Brinkley responded, wrongly of course, "I'm not on the air." He went on to call President Clinton a "bore." He said his victory speech was "one of the worst things I've ever heard."

"I thought we had signed off," Brinkley later **conceded**. "I thought I was not on the air." Brinkley later apologized to President Clinton when he was interviewing him on television. "What I said at the end of our election night coverage was both impolite and unfair, and I'm sorry. I regret it," Brinkley said. The president told him he understood how it could have happened. "I've said a lot of things myself late at night when I was tired, and you had really been through a rough day," President Clinton said. "I always believe you have to judge people on their whole work, and if you get judged based on your whole work, you come out way ahead." Still, Brinkley probably wished that he had just checked the mike before speaking!

A President's Joke That Backfired

President Ronald Reagan also had an unfortunate microphone mishap. Reagan was president from 1981 to 1989, during the cold war between the Soviet Union and the United States. Both countries were developing some of the most destructive weapons ever known and claimed to have them ready to fire at any moment. People thought the **ominous** situation between the two countries could lead to World War III. President Reagan called the Soviet Union "the focus of evil in the modern world." It was a scary time to live through.

President Reagan was known as the Great Communicator because he could talk easily to people and knew how to make them laugh. One of his jokes, however, turned out not to be so funny. It was August 1984. President Reagan was testing a microphone before his weekly radio address. He had the **misfortune** of thinking the microphone was off. "My fellow Americans, I am pleased to tell you I just signed legislation which outlaws Russia forever," President Reagan suddenly announced. "The bombing begins in 5 minutes!"

It's a good thing the Soviet government didn't take President Reagan's words seriously. "All right, I shouldn't have said that," President Reagan later told reporters. He was **frustrated** that the news about his joke had been spread around the world.

In his last four years in office, President Reagan became friends with the new Soviet leader, Mikhail Gorbachev. In 1986, the two leaders met in Iceland to discuss eliminating all nuclear weapons. It was the beginning of the end of the cold war, which finally came to a complete end in 1991.

Take That, Mickey Mouse!

At least President Reagan didn't make fun of a U.S. idol. Nancy Kerrigan made that mistake. Kerrigan was a famous Olympic figure skater. In 1994, she skated in the Winter Olympics in Norway and took second place. She won a silver medal. Winning a silver medal was a wonderful outcome for Kerrigan, considering she almost didn't make it to the Olympics. Just weeks earlier on January 6, 1994, Kerrigan was struck on the knee by a man with a metal baton at the U.S. National Skating Championships. The man was a friend of a rival champion skater, Tonya Harding. Harding later confessed to knowing all about the **treacherous** plan to hurt Kerrigan.

There was a lot of sympathy for Kerrigan. She had to train in a swimming pool for the next several weeks. Both she and Harding made the Olympic team. Harding was allowed to compete in the Olympics because at that time no one knew she was involved in the attack. Skating fans cheered for Kerrigan and hoped she would be able to win a medal. On February 23, 1994, Kerrigan won her silver medal. The United States loved her! She was known as America's Sweetheart.

Her image wouldn't remain perfect for long, though. Kerrigan had a couple of embarrassing moments that tarnished her image. First, while waiting to receive her silver medal onstage at the Olympics, Kerrigan made a comment about the gold medalist, Oksana Baiul. Baiul was fixing her makeup before the awards ceremony. "Oh, come on," Kerrigan said, not realizing her microphone was on. "So she's going to get out here and cry again. What's the difference?" Oops. Maybe Kerrigan wasn't as perfect as she seemed to be.

Then, to celebrate her win, Kerrigan appeared in homecoming parades in the United States. People loved to see her and get her autograph. Like many Olympic winners who also have interesting personalities, Kerrigan was offered money from companies to

Nancy Kerrigan teamed up with Mickey Mouse after her Olympic victory.

promote their products. The Walt Disney Company gave Kerrigan $2 million! She was hired to promote all of Disney's products. Disney executives also wanted her to appear in their parade at Walt Disney World®. Kerrigan actually left the closing ceremonies at the Olympics to be in the Disney parade.

On February 27, 1994, Kerrigan rode on a fire truck in the Disney parade. She was **escorted** by Mickey Mouse. The fans loved her, but Kerrigan apparently wasn't so thrilled to be sitting next to Mickey Mouse. She didn't realize the microphone she was wearing was turned on when she called the whole thing "corny."

"This is so dumb," she was overheard saying. "I hate it. This is the most corny thing I have ever done." Poor Mickey! Kerrigan was embarrassed. She said later that she was actually talking about her mom's insistence that she wear her silver medal. She said she didn't want it to "look like bragging." She said the parade had been fun. "Riding down Main Street with Mickey Mouse? What could be better than that?" she asked.

Chapter 5
Caught On Camera

Cameras are everywhere. With reality shows videotaping people's everyday lives, cell phones with built-in cameras, and home video cameras, it's hard for anyone to live life without having some of his or her embarrassing moments recorded on camera.

The television show *America's Funniest Home Videos* has been a popular show for more than a decade. People send the show videotapes of embarrassing things that have happened to them. For example, a videotape might show someone's pants falling down in public or someone looking ridiculous as he imitates a celebrity. The secret of the show's success is that people continue to have their embarrassing moments recorded on camera and are willing to expose these moments to a national television audience.

Now just imagine what it might feel like to be an important or famous person caught doing something really embarrassing on camera. Even though important or famous people are always in the spotlight, they occasionally do something they would not normally do in public. It must be an **ominous** feeling knowing that if you do something embarrassing, there will be a good chance a camera is watching.

What happens when famous people are caught on camera doing something embarrassing? Sometimes the **consequences** are slight, but at other times they are very serious. As one national political figure learned, even small mistakes can have a major impact on a politician's career.

A Big Spelling Mistake

A button pokes fun of Dan Quayle for his spelling mistake.

Former Vice President Dan Quayle didn't just misspeak on camera, he misspelled! Dan Quayle was the vice president under President George H. W. Bush from 1989 to 1993. He was 41 when he became vice president. On June 15, 1992, Quayle attended a spelling bee at the Luis Munoz-Rivera School in Trenton, New Jersey. Reporters were there, too, with television cameras to record the visit. Vice President Quayle asked 12-year-old William Figueroa to spell the word *potato*. The sixth-grader walked to the chalkboard and wrote *p-o-t-a-t-o*. The vice president told Figueroa that he had made a mistake and asked him to add an *e* on the end of the word.

"I knew he was wrong," Figueroa later told comedian David Letterman. "But since he's the vice president, I went back and put an *e* on and went back to my seat." **Unfortunately** for Vice President Quayle, it turned out that Figueroa was the one who was right. The word *potato* doesn't have an *e* on the end.

Even before the spelling bee, critics had given Quayle a hard time because of his youth and inexperience. The spelling mistake put him in **treacherous** political territory. Jokes about the misspelled word quickly spread.

Vice President Quayle **conceded** he had made a spelling error, but he said the flashcard he was holding at the spelling bee had the word *potato* misspelled. Still, Quayle suffered dire **consequences**. His political career was never quite the same afterward.

Queens Are Human, Too!

Elizabeth II, the queen of England, is on television all of the time. Whenever she leaves her home, a gang of photographers follows her every move. She must be on her best behavior at all times. Whatever she says and does in public is photographed or videotaped.

Queen Elizabeth is currently the head of England's royal family. Hundreds of years ago, the royal family was in charge of running the government of England. The kings and queens of England were very powerful. A lot has changed since those days. Today, the queen is the symbolic leader of the people of England, Scotland, Northern Ireland, and Wales. The queen of England does not run the government. The prime minister, who is an elected official, runs the government.

Even though members of the royal family do not have political power, they are still very important people. The members of the royal family are supposed to set an example for the people of England and the other countries in the United Kingdom. Good manners— especially in public—are very important to Queen Elizabeth. When members of the royal family appear in public, many people look to see how they are dressed and how they are behaving. Members of the royal family represent the United Kingdom to the whole world.

So it was a big deal when the queen was caught on camera picking her nose! She was being driven to a public event, wearing her white gloves and all. The camera caught her with her finger up her nose. Imagine the **considerable** embarrassment the queen must have felt in this situation. Even a queen can be caught doing something really embarrassing!

Chapter 6
Sports Bloopers

Have you ever been in a sports event and missed a ball or struck out? Were you embarrassed? How did you handle it? Usually, the coach will tell you to "be a good sport" about it and just take it in stride. It's still pretty embarrassing though. Imagine you did something like that when the stakes were a lot higher. Imagine you did something embarrassing in a really big championship game. Also imagine that what you did caused your team to lose the big game. How do you think you would feel in that situation?

The history of sports is filled with **dramatic** moments and embarrassing ones as well. Professional players make a lot of money and compete at the highest levels. Millions of fans watch their every move. When a player does something spectacular, the fans roar in approval. When a player does something wrong, the fans may get very upset.

What if the mistake costs the team a big game? It's hard to imagine that a star player could mess up a really big play or miss a ball. We sometimes think that professional players should always know what they're doing and never make a mistake. Are these expectations realistic, though?

Even the most talented sports heroes are capable of messing up every now and then. Do you think they suffer from intense embarrassment afterward? Read on to learn about the embarrassing playing errors of several professional athletes.

Don't Let It Happen Again!

Leon Lett was selected to play professional football for the Dallas Cowboys in 1991. By the 1993 season, Lett was coming into his own as a player. That year, however, he fractured his ankle in the third game and was forced to sit out until Thanksgiving Day 1993.

On that day, Lett was playing defensive tackle in a game against the Miami Dolphins. It was a strange day in Dallas, Texas. The weather was unusually cold and snowy, so the field was **treacherous**. The Cowboys were winning 14–13 when the Miami Dolphins made a last-second field-goal attempt. If the kick was good, the Dolphins would win the game 16–14. The field-goal kick was from the 41-yard line. It was a tough play because of the snowy conditions.

A Cowboys player blocked the kick. All the Dallas Cowboys had to do was avoid touching the ball, and they would win the game. Suddenly, Lett began running straight for the ball. His teammates called out "Peter!" which was the Cowboys' code for "stay away from the ball." Lett didn't seem to hear his teammates' warnings. He slid on the ice and right into the ball on the 7-yard line. Instead of covering the football, Lett pushed the ball toward the end zone. Then, a player for the Dolphins jumped on the ball at the 1-yard line and slid into the end zone. Lett's mistake gave the Miami Dolphins another chance to kick a field goal. Lett sat on the sideline filled with **anguish** as the Dolphins then kicked a field goal to win the game.

The play was caught on camera and replayed over and over. Lett will never live down that day. "It's part of NFL history," Cowboys assistant coach Joe Avezzano said.

Buckner's Blunder

Before the Boston Red Sox won the World Series championship in 2004, they had not won the World Series since 1918. Red Sox fans had been **frustrated** by this fact for many years. In 1986, the team found itself leading the New York Mets three games to two in the World Series. One more Red Sox win and the Red Sox would win the World Series. In Game 6, the Red Sox took a 3–1 lead over the Mets in the tenth inning. Now only three outs separated the Red Sox from the World Series title. When the first two Mets batters made outs, the Red Sox and their fans were ready to celebrate. All they needed was one out.

Suddenly, the Mets rallied. The Mets tied the game with three straight hits. The potential winning runner stood on second. Mets batter Mookie Wilson hit a routine ground ball to Red Sox first baseman Bill Buckner. Somehow Bill Buckner missed the ball. As the ball trickled into the outfield, the winning runner scored. Nobody could believe that Buckner had missed the ground ball.

The Red Sox went on to lose Game 7 of the series to the Mets. Still, all anyone could talk about after the 1986 World Series was Bill Buckner's **dismal** mistake. It couldn't have happened at a worse moment.

Here's Bill Buckner right after his big sports blunder. How do you think he's feeling? →

It's Not Over Yet!

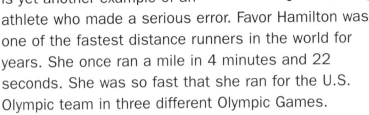

Suzy Favor Hamilton is yet another example of an athlete who made a serious error. Favor Hamilton was one of the fastest distance runners in the world for years. She once ran a mile in 4 minutes and 22 seconds. She was so fast that she ran for the U.S. Olympic team in three different Olympic Games.

In February 1994, Favor Hamilton was competing in a one-mile race at an indoor track-and-field meet in Fairfax, Virginia. Favor Hamilton had a good chance of winning, but she was going up against the 1992 Olympic 1,500-meter winner from Algeria, Hassiba Boulmerka. Five thousand people had packed the field house to see the big race.

On an indoor track, a mile is eight laps. Boulmerka was in the lead as the runners started the last two laps of the race. Suddenly, Favor Hamilton started to make her move. Favor Hamilton surged into the lead during the seventh lap. She raced to what she thought was the finish line and stopped. She thought that the race was over and that she had won! **Unfortunately**, she had one more lap to go.

Favor Hamilton later **conceded** that she had lost count of the laps. "I took a deep breath," she recalls, "and they whizzed by. Out of the corner of my eye I saw them. It was the weirdest feeling. I wanted to tell everybody to stop so that I could jump back in the race."

Favor Hamilton learned a lesson from that embarrassing loss. "I'm just going to chalk this up to good experience," she said back in 1994. Her mistake certainly hasn't kept her off the track. As she continues her career, Favor Hamilton probably will make sure she keeps track of the number of laps she has run!

Des Walker is on the ground after his unfortunate head shot. Walker's teammates know he's made a big mistake!

That's the Wrong Goal, Des!

The soccer player Des Walker's mistake cost his team a championship. In England, soccer is called football and it's really popular. In 1991, Des Walker was on the team from Nottingham Forest, England. His team was playing in a football championship against a team from Tottenham, near London, England.

More than 80,000 fans gathered in a stadium in Wembley, England, on May 18, 1991, to see Nottingham Forest go up against the Tottenham Spurs. More than 600 million people were watching the game on television, in about 100 countries. All eyes were on Walker. He was a star player known to be one of the fastest players on defense.

The championship game went into overtime with the score tied, 1 to 1. The next goal would win the championship for one team—and lose it for the other. In overtime, the ball soared toward Walker, who was near his team's goal.

Walker was trying to get the ball away from his team's goal. He headed the ball, hoping to send it out of bounds. The ball made contact with Walker's head. WHAM! He headed the ball into the net, right past his own teammate—the goalkeeper who was defending Nottingham Forest's goal. Walker must have been **petrified**. He had scored the winning goal for the other team! As a **consequence**, the Tottenham Spurs won the game and England's football championship.

At the time, the loss was very hard for Nottingham Forest fans to accept. Walker's fans were **anguished** by the play, too. Still, Walker wouldn't allow this one mistake to stop him from playing the game he loved. Walker continued to play soccer until he retired in May 2004 at the age of 38. Walker is remembered as one of the best defenders in the league.

Everybody Feels Embarrassed Now and Then

Embarrassing moments can happen to anyone at any time. You may have thought you were the only one to ever do anything embarrassing. Now you see that even famous people have to deal with embarrassing moments. They trip over themselves. They sometimes can't spell. Political figures, pop stars, sports stars, and even queens would have to **concede** that embarrassing moments can be hysterical—especially if those moments happen to someone else.

Feeling embarrassed doesn't have to be a major **ordeal**. We can learn to laugh at our own embarrassing situations. We can also encourage other people to laugh at theirs. After all, feeling embarrassed sometimes is just a part of life for everyone!

GLOSSARY

absorbed in a state in which something takes up all of your attention. **Absorbing** means taking something in.

absurd ridiculous or unreasonable

anguish pain or torment. **Anguished** means tormented or in great pain.

arise to come about or to happen

conceded admitted or confessed. **Conceded** also means awarded, granted, or compromised.

consequences effects or results

considerable large in amount. **Considerable** also means important. **Considerably** means quite or much.

crisis a time of great danger. **Crises** is the plural of **crisis**.

destined determined beforehand by some unseen force

dismal gloomy or depressing

dramatic sensational or spectacular. **Dramatic** also means relating to the theater.

escorted accompanied, led, or showed the way

frustrated prevented from attaining a goal. **Frustrated** also means feeling discouraged.

imaginative having the ability to create new images or ideas

immersed buried deeply in something

implied suggested but not stated directly

insurance a way of guaranteeing protection against something bad happening. An **insurance** policy is a contract that offers to pay money to someone in case of an important loss or injury.

misfortune bad luck

momentarily happening for a very short time

noticeably in a way that clearly attracts attention

ominous threatening or menacing

ordeal a situation that is difficult to get through

perpetual continuing forever

persistence the quality that allows you to continue doing something no matter what happens. **Persisted** means a person kept doing something in spite of problems or obstacles.

petrify to scare or frighten. **Petrifying** means very frightening or scary.

regret feeling sorry for something you did or said

rival a person competing with you for something that you want. A **rivalry** is a competition.

strengthened made stronger

subtlety the quality of being very faint or indirect

supposedly believed or considered likely to be true

treacherous dangerous, undependable, or disloyal

unfortunately unhappily or unluckily

INDEX